David Young

The Humbugs of Niagara Falls exposed

David Young

The Humbugs of Niagara Falls exposed

ISBN/EAN: 9783743340299

Manufactured in Europe, USA, Canada, Australia, Japa

Cover: Foto ©ninafisch / pixelio.de

Manufactured and distributed by brebook publishing software
(www.brebook.com)

David Young

The Humbugs of Niagara Falls exposed

THE

HUMBUGS

—OF—

Niagara Falls

EXPOSED.

—WITH—

A Complete Tourists' Guide,

THE HUMBUGS

OF

NIAGARA FALLS,

EXPOSED.

——— ✳ ———

NIAGARA FALLS has been noted for its HUMBUGS as far back as the days of "SAM PATCH". For when according to announcement the day had arrived for him to make his great leap from a scaffold placed at the foot of Goat Island, into the boiling waters below the Falls and the expectant crowd had assembled they were coolly informed that "Sam" had broken his leg and consequently would be unable to jump until the next day. The people forgot their disappointment out of pure sympathy for "Sam's" misfortune, and remained all night at the hotels and boarding houses, and only became conscious of the duplicity practiced upon them when their bills were presented next morning, too late for material service. Those who remained and those who arrived the next day were surprised to see "Sam" walking without crutches, and also making his fearful leap into the gorge below. The most miraculous healing of a broken limb on record!

At other times flaming announcements are sent out over all the country that a boat con-

taining bears and other animals would be sent
down the river, and thousands would come to
witness the fearful plunge over the Falls, only
to behold an old scow lodge in the shallow rapids above the Falls. or the broken splinters of
the old tub dash through the foaming waters
and disappear over the precipice. A "Buffalo
Hunt" is announced, real wild buffaloes from
the Western plains are to be turned loose in a
large enclosure, and Buffalo Bill. assisted by a
company o' plainsmen from the far-west, are to
delineate the excitement of a real Buffalo hunt.
The crowd assemble to witness a great treat of
a most exciting kind only to see a couple of old,
decrepit buffaloes from the Museum Gardens
lazily feeding on the green pastures of the old
Drummondville race course and Buffalo Bill
and his braves decked in gay trappings riding
about the course. Several attempts are made
to excite the buffaloes into a run; but all the
flogging, clubbing and prodding fail to devel-
op a speed in the monarchs of the prairie above
a trot. Finally the "brave hunters" turn their
attention to a few Texan steers, which had been
secured from a passing train for the occasion,
and after a great effort actually succeeded in
getting them to run from their pursuers.

Thus it has ever been, and in proportion as
stately hotels have arisen from the modest log
or frame houses of the early days, so humbug-
ism has increased. Swindling has become
more systematic than in former days, and the
public will be surprised when they find who
are connected with it. It is gradually driving
visitors from the place, and has given Niagara
Falls a name not to be coveted by the poorest

hamlet in Christendom.   For instance, a gentleman arrives at Niagara Falls and puts up at
one of the principal hotels and depends upon
his Host for directions in visiting the various
points of interest in the vicinity.   He naturally
expects reliable information, but the chances
are he will be deceived.   It may be and often is
the case, that some one in connection with the
hotel is connected with one or more of the
points of interest on either or both sides of the
river.   He goes to the office and asks for information concerning the points of interest, and
there, only such points as are in the interest of
the hotel or of those connected with the hotel,
are pointed out to him as points of interest visited by the great multitude, while all other
points are represented as not being worth the
time go and see.

Immediately he is put into a hack, the driver
mounts his seat, and the individual has really
commenced his sight-seeing.   The driver who
knows his business as well as the pedagogue
knows his multiplication table, plies his victim,
no, not his victim, but the victim of mine host,
with marvellous narrations of the events and
occurrences that have taken place at those
points which they intend visiting, thus drawing
the man's mind away from other points that
the driver knows he dare not drive to on pain of
INSTANT DISMISSAL.   Should the gentleman
mention any other point, he is promptly dis-
couraged, is told that the place is not worth
seeing or that it is not safe to visit, and should
he still insist upon going, the driver would be
compelled, point blank, to refuse to take him,
and should the party yet persist in going he

would have to walk or procure another hack.

For the purpose of illustrating this fact, we will give a single instance: Some time in September, 1882, there was a Druggists' Convention held at Niagara Falls N. Y., the delegates putting up at one of the principal hotels, and during their stay wished to visit the Whirlpool and Whirlpool Rapids on the American side; to their astonishment, when they wished to be driven to those places, the hackmen connected with the hotel refused to take them, and they were compelled to employ other hackmen to drive them where they desired to go.

Sometimes a contract is entered into between the manager of some point or points of interest and the proprietor of a hotel, in which he agrees for a certain amount of money to drive as many of the guests of the hotel as possible to the particular point or points, as the case may be. In such a case the driver is in danger of losing his position if he does not go there.

A certain driver was reprimanded for not driving into Prospect Park as often as he should have done for the interest of his employer, so when the next man entered his hack and asked where he was going to take him he was answered, "Into Prospect Park, sir." "But I do not want to go there," said the stranger. "I will take you there whether you want to go or not, sir," said the driver, and he did take him there. By this private arrangement other hackmen are not permitted to go on the premises of these hotels to solicit, and the stranger is thus left at the mercy of a grinding monopoly The "outside hackmen" as they are called, would give their services for much less, are just as

obliging and equally as trustworthy as are those
·"ho are supposed to be in connection with the
ho el. As to the que s·ion of safety there is no
u.uference between an "outside" and an "inside"
hackman; there is the honorable and dishonor-
able among both classes. But where imposition
is attempted the stranger can obtain sure and
speedy redress by following the instructions
given in the chapter "How to avoid being hum-
bugged."

COMMISSION FRAUDS.

—o:⊙:o—

T HE commission system of doing business is now probably the most
fruitful source of complaint at Niag-
ara. The Falls is a place of magnificent distances and strangers are drawn from place to place
by obliging and condescending hackmen.
These apparently disinterested and self-sacrific-
ing individuals are always ready, willing, and
waiting to advise new-comers upon any subject
pertaining to the locality. It is natural that
strangers should fall into their hands. It is
their business to deal with strangers in this particular.

They pay for the privilege of doing so. They
are protected by the by-laws and ordinances of
the municipalities on both sides of the river in
the plying of their vocation. Strangers un-
acquaint ;d with the neighborhood, are compelled to ask fc r direction, and nothing can be
more natural than they should seek information
from those commissioned to give it, and who
are most accessible and most willing to comply

with their requests. In the very nature of things this must continue to be so while the transportation business of the neighborhood is in the hands of the Hack Fraternity. Now, hackmen, like other people, work for money, and while they appear to talk in the interest of the stranger applying to them for information they have their principal eye on their own interests and only recommend such movements as will result in turning them an "honest penny." Hackmen look upon strangers only as so much stock in trade, and as soon as thay have made out of them the last margin of profit they want to see them no more. It is a fact that at nearly all points of interest about Niagara Falls, hackmen get a commission from the keepers of the points for bringing strangers to them. The fraud is in this: A stranger paying 50 cents for the privilege of visiting a point of interest, possibly feels that he has received the worth of his money and has no thought that a fraud has been practiced upon him. The frand is perpetrated all the same. The keeper of the point demands the 50 cents ostensibly for the privilege while the fact is, the keeper is demand ing 25 cents for the privilege of seeing the point, and 25 cents to pay the hackman for bringing the victim there. The 50 cents is obtained by falsely pretending that it is wholly for the privilege of viewing the point of interest, when the fact is one half of it is demanded for the hackman and is handed to him as soon as the stranger's back is turned.

The following table shows the prices charged for admission to the points of interest about Niagara Falls, and the manner in which the

charges collected are divided between the keepers of the points and the hackmen:

CANADA SIDE.

POINTS OF INTEREST.	AMOUNT CHARGED.	AMOUNT PAID TO HACKMEN.
Whirlpool............:.........	$0.50	.... $0.25
Whirlpool Rapids......	50	 25
Museum...............	50	 25
Under sheet of water at Table Rock...........	1.00	 50
Burning Spring........	50	 25
Crossing Upper Suspen- sion Bridge on foot...	25	 00
Two horse Carriage....	50	 00
One horse Carriage.....	37½	 00

AMERICAN SIDE.

Prospect Park and In- clined Railway......	50	 25
Shadow of the Rock....	1 00	 50
Goat Island..........	50	 00
Cave of the Winds......	1.00	 50
Whirlpool Rapids......	50	 25
Whirlpool.............	50	 25

At nearly all of these points of interest there
are fancy goods stores and an army of persist-
saleswomen. Of all the money invested in
articles there offered for sale the accompanying
hackman gets 25 per cent as his commission for
furnishing the customer. In addition to the
commissions paid, keepers of points of interest
in many cases subsidize Hack Associations with
large bonuses and individual hackmen with ex-
travagant presents. In return for the commissions, and the subsidies and the presents, the
hackmen talk strangers into "taking in" the
points from which they derive their commissions, subsidies and presents. Some hackmen

are subsidized by one point and some by another. In all this the stranger is the victim. It is he that furnishes the capital to run Niagara and to run it, too, with all the peculiarities that characterize the place.

Now what is the remedy? Is it possible to avoid the impositions? When people come to Niagara their object is to see the Falls. They possibly don't know anything about the Devil's Hole or most of the other outlying points of inter est so extensively extolled by the generous Cabby As soon, however, as they get seated in a conveyance they are driven to the point farthest from the Falls—a point on all occasions where commission is paid. This seen another is visited, and then another, and last of all the object of the visit, a view of the Falls. On the Canada side this is free consequently commissionless, hence it is quite apparent why the hackmen should take his party last of all to the point he most desired to visit. One remedy would be for strangers to refuse to be drawn to any point or place where commissions are paid to hackmen. This would have a tendency to do away with the commission system and necessarily render hackmen a degree more disinterested, and possibly a degree more honest in their representations to strangers.

Another course, but somewhat more complicated would, in a measure accomplish the desired resut. Let the stranger in bargaining with his hackman, arrange before starting upon a round of sight-seeing, that the hackman is to be satisfied with the fee agreed upon alone, for the drive, and that the stranger is to receive all "Commissions" paid at the different points.

Take an example, and see how the parties interested will stand at the end of the trip. A party of four engage a hack to go to all the points of interest for $5. The first point visited say, is goat Island. Now the party visiting pays $2. No commission is paid. The hackman would under ordinary circumstances get nothing and the party according to the arrangement made gets nothing back. While upon the Island they take in the Cave of the Winds. There they pay $1 each, and by the terms of their agreement each gets back 50 cents. They next go to Prospect Park, they pay 50 cents each and each get back 25 cents commission. They next visit the Whirlpool Rapids on the American side and pay 50 cents each, receiving back 25 cents each. They then cross the lower bridge, and pay in the shape of bridge toll $1.50 of which nothing is received in return. They then take in Whirlpool Rapids on the Canadian side and the Whirlpool paying $1 each, for the two, and receive back as commission 50 cents. each. The museum, and the Burning Springs entail another dollar outlay, and adds 50 cents to the receipts of each on commission account. They now return to the American side by the upper bridge paying $1.50 for that privilege, out of which they get no return. Let us see now how the account stands.

Paid for hack hire..........	......	$5.00
Paid at Goat Island........	......	2.00
Paid at Cave of the Winds..	......	4.00
Received in return........	$2.00	
Paid at Prospect Park......	......	2.00
Received in return........	1.00	.
Paid at Whirlpool Rapids,		
(American side)........	......	2.00

Received in return	1.00	
Paid at Lower Bridge		1.50
Paid at Whirlpool Rapids (Canada side)		2.00
Received in return	1.00	
Paid at Whirlpool		2.00
Received in return	1.00	
Paid at Burning Springs		2.00
Received in return	1.00	
Paid at Museum		2.00
Received in return	1.00	
Paid for crossing Up. Bridge		1.50
Toll, stone road, Canada side		0.10
	$8.00	$26.10

By this arrangement the party has the use of the hack for nothing and 75 cts each to the good; have practically paid half rates for visiting all the points. By this example it will be readily seen that the amount paid to hackmen, as hack hire direct, is only a small part of their gains. The driver, in this case, without the special arrangement spoken of, could have well afforded to drive the party for nothing, relying upon the commission for his remuneration.

The following case came under the observation of the writer in the summer of 1882, and only illustrates the rule at Niagara Falls. A party of six gentlemen, out for a drive, engaged a hackman for six dollars to take them to the principal points of interest. They took in everything recommended by the generous driver, and the trip cost them for tolls $33.00 out of which the driver pocketed $12.00 as his share of the spoils, thus netting by the transaction $18.00 and was ready for a like trip in the afternoon. When they landed, the young gentlemen not knowing that the driver had pocketed about half the amount they had paid, handed him a further tip of 25 cents each, in consideration of the good-natured amusement he had afforded them during the engagement. Is there no fraud in this? Would these young gentlemen have dealt with the driver upon such terms had they been aware of the real facts? They were paying him as they supposed for his services in the $6. They were not aware that they had paid him twice over that in another way before their journey ended. The hackmen alone could not thus prey upon the travelling public; but the combination that exists between them and the dealers on every hand, is such that the stranger unassisted is not able to contend with. (The following case also, came within the writer's observation during the summer of 1882. A hackman got a party of six ladies into his carriage, at the Great Western Railway Station, to be taken to the Falls, for 10 cents each. When he got to the Falls he said to the ladies "you may as well sit still and go on up to the Burning Springs, it won't cost you any more." After some solicitation the ladies accepted the hackman's apparently generous offer, and were driven to the place indicated. All went well until they were to leave, when they were met with a demand for $3.00, and despite all their protestations the money had to be paid. Out of this plunder the hackman got $1.50. This is only a further example of the rule at Niagara Falls.) The travelling public have the remedy in their hands. Will they ever apply it, or will they go on as they have for the last thirty years, submitting to the impositions practiced, and leaving the place with anything but pleasant memories? The authorities in the neighborhood of the Falls will never remedy the grievances. They are too much in the power of those who profit by the peculiar system complained of. A free park and a street railroad on both sides of the river would do much to bring back to this much persecuted locality the good name that now seems permantly lost to it. This, like any other reform at Niagara, must come from without the limits of the area given over to the peculiar commercial morality that characterizes the place. Without the park there is no hope for reformation. With it a new system may be inaugurated and better days dawn upon the neighborhood.

HACKMEN'S TRICKS.

—o:◯:o—

HERE is probably no place in the world where there are so many opportunities for committing frauds and impositions as at this point. It would seem almost incredible that these fraud should continue to be repeated when all the world has been warned through the press against them. The very geography of the locality, the circumstances peculiar to the place, and the exigencies of the business people themselves tend to place strangers at the mercy of any who may desire to take advantage of them.

The Grand Trunk, (formerly the Great Western,) and the Erie Railways connect at Niagara Falls, Canada side. People going east by the Erie leave the Grand Trunk Railway at this point, and passing through the station, get into the Erie train. The following is one of the

tricks that have been played upon people chang-
ing cars here:(A stranger came out through the
station and enquired of the first person he met
(who by the way was a hackman) for the Erie
train. The hackman seeing that the stranger
was not posted said to him: "Get right into my
hack and I will take you to the station. You
have not a moment to spare—It will cost you
three dollars." The stranger not being aware
that he was then standing within a few feet of
the very train he was enquiring for, and fearful
of being late, acted upon the hackman's sugges-
tion, who deliberately then drove the stranger
away from the train he should have taken,
across the Suspension Bridge, where he had to
pay a further charge of 75 cents bridge toll, to
the Erie station on the American side.

Could heartless imposition be more flagrant!

A favorite trick of the lower grade of hackmen is to bring their patrons to the train they
wish to go by just about the time the train is to
start, and then demand from them probably
double the amount agreed upon, threatening the
interference of the police if the demand is not
satisfied. In nine cases out of ten the stranger
pays through fear of being detained.

Another trick is to keep whatever bills may
be handed them under these circumstances, in
payment of the fare refusing to hand back the
change. They know that in a few minutes the
stranger will be gone and there is an end to
the contention.

Parties to leave by train in this way are call
ed in hackmen's vernacular "train parties;" and
a hackman has a peculiar knack of finding out
what disposition his patrons are about to make

of themselves. A hackman seeing a stranger walking along the bank towards the Falls will drive near him and say "Going up to the Falls? The stranger says "yes." The hackman says "Get in, I'm going right up; it won't cost you anything." The stranger gets in and is driven to the Falls. Here he is entreated by a bevy of guides and runners to go under the sheet of water.

He consents, and for this disinterested act of kindness (?) he pays one dollar, fifty cents as commission to a person he never saw before and by whom he hopes never to be recognized again. And should the stranger happen to buy a quantity of fancy goods, or get his picture taken, the hackman gets his fee out of that also. Another trick is, if parties wish to go to the Whirlpool, the driver will be sure to drive to the Whirlpool Rapids first, and then, after they have paid their fifty cents, he will tell them that the Whirlpool is farther down the river. Or, if a party has a ticket for a certain point of interest they will be driven to some other place, which they suppose is the point for which their ticket calls, and are passed right through, but when they return they are compelled to pay fifty cents each. After this fleecing, if they are not too angry, and have time, they can go to the point for which they hold a ticket. Strangers are led to believe, by evasion and deceit on the part of some of the hackmen, that certain points of interest are free, when it is well know to the hackman that a fee is charged. The perpetration of this imposition is facilitated by the managers of the points referred to. The matter of charge is not mentioned as the party passes in, but the demand is made when they are about to leave. In many cases the party would not have visited the place at all if they had known that a charge would have been made, and particularly if they had known the amount charged. In all such cases the hackman gets his share of the money paid. It is this hope of reward that prompts him to delude and over reach the stranger. Practically the hackmen control all the lines of business peculiar to this locality. Whom they favor will succeed. Whom they desire to crush must come to grief. If in their dreadful might they set their face against a business man, the grass will grow at his threshold before a season passes. Therefore strangers would do well to go to no point of interest where hackmen get a commission, and into no fancy goods store where hackmen, or clerks, or porters importune them to go. At all such places the parties importuning get a commission on the amount sold, and the stranger is charged that much extra for what he buys.

HACKMEN NOT ALONE BAD.

——o:◯:o——

THUS we see that the hackmen are not the only ones at Niagara Falls that take advantage of the stranger. No sooner does a stranger appear who cannot pronounce the local "shibboleth" than all kinds of goods advance to three or four times their usual price. Cigars that cost a cent and a half each are sold for twenty cents. Lager beer goes up to ten cents a glass ; pop the same, and everything else in proportion. Ornaments that come from England are sold to the stranger as Table Rock ornaments, and fabulous stories are told of the difficulty experienced in procuring them. It is a wonder that some of the spokes of the 'bus that went down with Table Rock are not for sale in some of the shops ?

We find that there are some hackmen just as honest and upright in their vocation as other men are in their business. They try to make all they can : yet they do not deceive their parties, but tel them frankly what is charged at the various points of interest, and endeavor to give them reliable information. It is true that they also receive the commission, but as many of them receive but a few paltry dollars per month as wages, they are compelled to take the commission in order to support themselves and family, If owners of hacks would pay their drivers reasonable wages for their services very much of the fraud now practiced by them would disappear.

The Experience of John Lauderbauch.

—o:⊃:o—

"WELL, Mr. Lauderbauch, I hear that you have been to Niagara Falls and had a very good time. Will you please tell us all about it ?"

"Vell, mine friendt, it vas youst like dis. Mine frau Petsey, she say to me, Shon, you has vorked hard all der summer und der best is for you to shust shtop a leetle und rest mit yourself a vile."

"Vell," I say to mine Petsey, "vell, Petsey, vot

I shall do mit myself?"   "Vell," says Petsey,
" you go one ov dem excursions mit to der Falls
und have vone goot dimes, und bring me vone
new dress vhen you come back mit yourself."

"So I vent right avay quick, und got me vone
of does excursion dickets, und der next morning
I got der stheam vagon in, und putty soon der
bell he ring, und den der vagon he sthart off und,
Shiminy cripes, you ought youst to see how
dem vences und dem pig stables, und dem hen
houses und such things did fly py.   I daut dot
efery dings vas alife.   Ven ve der Falls am to,
und der vagon got out, eferypody vas hollering
youst so loud vat he could, und vhen he say
'Free buss,' for some davern vot I don't under-
sthandt. So, says I myself to, 'Shon, dot is der
blace vor you.'   So I got der buss in, und ve
drove der sthreet drough, und putty quick ve
come to der davern ven der bus sthopped, und
I got mit myself out und valked der house in
und sit down myself.   Putty soon a man comes
und says dot dinner vas ready, did I vant some?
und I say yes.   Und den I got up and veut der
dable to und sit myself down, und eating commenced.   I dook a cup of coffee und I put dree
sphocnsful ov sugar in, because I daught it
vould not cost any more ov I put in dree sphoon-
fulls as vone.   I eat a schmall biece of meat,
und some botaters, und ven I vas done I asked
der davern-keeper vot it all cost, und he said
'vone tollar.'   So tinks I, by Shiminy, dare bees
vone tollar gone putty quick.   Vell, I says, here
bees your tollar, und now I bees going to look
aroundt some.   Vell, says der man vhat der
davern keeps, don't you vant ter ride ?   Oh, no,
I says, I can aroundt valk.   O, no, said der man

vhat der davern keeps, dot vill never do; you only go der vorld vonce drough, und so may youst so goot ride as valk. Vell, I says, how mooch it cost ven I ride mit der vagon roundt? O, he say, ve make dot all richt ven you back comes. So I say all richt. So I got der vagon in, und der man vhat sit on der top of der vagon he starts off mit me right avay quick."

"Vell, der first blace vhat ve sthopped at vas dot long pridge vhat goes der river ofer, und a man comes out und says dot I must give him vone tollar pefore I goes der pridge over. Vell, I gives der man vone tollar, und den we vent on der oder side, und vent der river down dill we comes to a blace vhere a man comes und opens der vagon door und asks me to get out. So I gets out und goes der house in vhere every dings looks very nice, und vone man he dakes me und sits ve in a vagon mit a box pelow vhich dey full of vater mikes; und den vhen der box vas full of vater avay der ding vent, und der firsht ding dot I knowed I vas down the river pank, vhen a man comes and says dot he musht my bicture dake. Vell, I said, if he musht he musht, for I could not help it. So in a leedle vhile he comes und says dot he must hive five tollars. Und I say for vhat? Und he says for dem bictures. So I gives him fife tollars for dem bictures vhich I hafe not seen; but der man says it bees all right und he vill send me dem bictures putty soon right avay quick."

"So I vent und got in dot vagon again, und a poy he comes und pulls der rope vhat makes der pell ring for der ding to go, und den he vants fifty cents. So I gites dot poy fifty cents, und dinks myself dot de money flies avay putty

quick. But vhen I got up to der top again I vas
vorser off as efer, for den der vimen dey comes
und say, puy dis und puy dot for to dake home
to mine Petsey. So I pought all I could in
my bockets carry, for vhich I pait ten tollars.
Den I stharted for der vagon, but von voman she
say sthop; you must fifty cents bay. Und I say
vhat for? Und she say for riding dot railway
down vhat mit vater goes. So I paid dem fifty
cents und got der vagon in. Den dar man vhat
sits on top he drife off putty quick, und vhen he
sthop again an oder man he opens der vagon
door und say 'Vhirlpool.' So I gets out ov der
vagon und I valks quite a long vay vhen I comes
to a blace vhere der vas some leedle vagons on
top of some dings vhat looked like a rail vence
tied fasht mit some ropes, apout as pig as der
lines vat mine Petsey hang her clothes on vhen
she vashes. I don't vas like der look of dose
dings, und say to dhis man, vat beesh dey?
Vhat vould pecome ov me ov dem ropes vould
preak in two pieces? Vell, der man he only laff
und say, dot depents vat kind ov a man you bees.
Vell, says I, I bees not a very pad man, und so I
got dot leedle vagon in und down I vent putty
quick. But I can dold you, mine frient, dot I
surely dought I vould go right dot rifer in. So
I not sthay long, but goes pack to der vagon
right avay quick; und ven I comes dare anudder
man he say, fifty cents, blease. So I not say
anydings but gifes him der fifty cents, und
dought to mineself dot if I did not got home putty
quick I vould not hafe monish enough left to
buy my Petsey a new dress. So I get der vagon
vone once more in, und der man vhat sits on top
ov der vagon he say, ve vill now go und see der

dable on der rock, or some dings like dot, und I
say all right. Vell, vhen ve comes dare I could
see no dable, noddings but some rock, so dought
ve vould go on. But a man he comes und says
you musht down mit der stairs go. So I say all
right. So he made me put on some close vhat
looked like some old sturgin skins, und den
der man he goes down firsht und I go pehind,
und putty quick ve comes to der blace vhere der
vater down comes vorser den at old Pill Powers'
saw mill. So ve not very long sthay, for I could
noddings but vater see any how. Den, ven I
back comes dere vas vone tollar to bay und den
der man vat with me vent down he vanted a
tollar for der use of dem old sturgin skin close,
vhich two tollars make. Und den dere vas
some more bictures vanted, but I begins to get
mat, so I dolt dem vellers dot dey musht go
mitout mine bicture. So I got der vagon once
more in, und der man vat sits on top he drifes
on putty fasht, und der firsht ding vhat I knowed ve comes to a place vhere der vas a leedle
fire plazing up, und der man vhat vas dare, he
too vanted a half tollar, und I said for vhat?
Vhen he said, for that fire looking at. So I gifes
him a half tollar, und delled him dot if he vould
come to see me I vould some prush heaps afire
make und he could see dot for noddings.

Den I dells der man vhat on top ov der vagon
sits to drife me pack der pridge over quicker as
no dime, for I not vant to see any more of der
Falls. But der man he say you must Prospect
Park see und some oder place vat dey calls Goat
Island. But I say it makes me noddings out, I
did not vant any more goats for to see for it cost
too many sthamps. Vell, dot bees all right, so

he drives me to der davern back, und der man
vhat der davern keeps he comes out und says,
vell, you hafe had vone good dimes I guess. O,
putty good, says I. Now, vat you vants for der
vagon? Twelve dollars, says der man. But,
my Shiminy, how dot makes my eyes stick out.
Und I say to der davern man, vat for so much?
Und he say, vell, look here, mine friendt, you
see der man vot sits on top of der vagon he dells
you how long der bridge vas over, und dot vas
vorth vone tollar; den he dells you how high
der pridge vas down, und dot vas vorth a tollar;
und den he tells you vhere der man falls der
pank ofer, und dot vas vone tollar wort; und he
exblained about der Maid dot vent der Mist
down, und dot vas vorth dree tollars; und den
der vagon vas vorth six tollars, so dot makes
der dwelve tollars. Vell, so I baid dem dwelve
tollars, und den der davern man say, come, my
friendt, have a trink mit me. Vell, I says, I
don't care if I do. So I dook a trink mit
him, und den I say, now hafe a trink mit me.
All right, he says, so den ve took anudder trink.
Den der davern man he say, now, look here,
my friendt, I have to bay for my trinks youst
as vell as you do, so now I vill schake der dice
mit you to see who shall poth trinks bay for.
So I say all right, und vhen ve had schook der
dice I had poth the trinks to bay for.

By dis dime I dought all vhat a man had to
do vhen at der Falls vas youst to give der beble
money. So vhen a poy comes up und asks my
poots for to shine I say yes, und I gifes him half
a tollar; und den anudder poy comes for to help
him, und he spit on der poots vone or twice, so
I gifes him half a tollar. Den one ov dem pig

plack fellers vhat come from der Sout, he comes und sthands and looks at me avhile, und as I hardly knowed if I was in der United States or Canada any more, so I gife him half a tollar too.

Und I can dold you py dis dhime my bocket pook looks putty slim, so I dake dot free bus for der stheam vagon house quicker as no dime, und I can dold you dot vhen I got dot stheam vagon vonce more in I feel petter as good. But vhen I gets home I dells Petsey dot I could findt no goot tress for her, und dot she musht vait dill ve dis fall our bigs kill.

A TRAVELLER'S PRAYER.

BY JOHN C. SHEA.

Oh, wonderful Niagara, amid thy ceaseless roar
The soul earth loosed and longing, to heaven would like to
   soar,
But viewing all thy beauties is satisfied to stay
If you'll send your hackmen and runners all away.
Yet it might be best to show them 'mong your other curious
   things ;
Let us think of that a moment, for the thought some laughter
   brings.
You might catalogue them fully, and regain from day to day –
The quarters that from visitors these men have taken away.
How would it do to place them where the 'Pool' goes round and
   round,
Mid the roar of rushing waters, sure some solace might be
   found.
And very soon the tables would be turned on men of sin,
For they, and not the traveller, would then be taken in.
But still there is another place their calling seems to suit,
Where clamors of their voice however loud would soon be mute,
And the visitor secure at rest, that rest he seldom finds,
Could smile to see their whips upraised from out the "Cave of
   Winds."
Another place is left for them ! And ever, ever more
The wrangling of the hackmen would be hushed along the
   shore,
Securely bound and numbered, and the place made free from
   toll—
Oh, what a place to jam them in would be the "Devil's Hole."

HOW TO SEE NIAGARA FALLS.

———o———

THE first and great object of the visitor to Niagara is to get a complete view of the Falls themselves. We shall therefore endeavor, as briefly as possible, to tell our readers how to see them.

The Grand Trunk Railway Station at Niagara Falls, Ont., (formerly Clifton,) is about two miles from the Falls on the Canada side. Visitors arriving at this station can engage hacks to take them to the Falls, or which is better still, if they have the time, they can take the walk along the beautiful river bank where a picturesque scenery is constantly presented to the eye until suddenly the Falls themselves burst upon the view and they are beheld in all their grandeur, free of charge.

A substantial iron fence along the edge of the bank was erected during the summer of 1883 by the Ontario Government, making this charming walk perfectly safe; also a sidewalk extending the whole distance to the Falls will be built by the town ready for the summer of 1884, which will complete what will ever after be the most delightful promenade on the continent.

Passengers coming from the west by the Michigan Central (Canada Southern) should leave the cars at the Niagara Falls station, where a short walk down to the river will bring them within full view of the mighty cataract.

Passengers arriving at Niagara Falls from any point on the American side can see the Falls from either Prospect Park or Goat Island.) Admission fee to Goat Island is 50 cents. This fee includes the Three Sister Islands, Biddle Stairs which leads down to the water's edge below the bank, and all the points that can be visited from Goat Island, except Cave of the Winds.

The admission to Prospect Park is 25 cents, the inclined railway leading down to the water's edge below the bank is 25 cents more, and the ferry to Canada also 25 cents. But parties wishing to go to Canada this way should purchase their ticket at the gate where 50 cts. will procure them a ticket that will admit to the Park and secure the use of the inclined railway, ferriage to Canada and return.

Or they can cross the new Suspension Bridge by paying 25 cents each way and 50 cents carriage toll.

But for those who study economy and wish at the same time to get a perfect and full view of the wonderful Niagara, the best way is to take the street car to Suspension Bridge for which the fare is only five cents, see the new Cantilever Bridge, then buy a return ticket over the Suspension Bridge, which is only 25 cents for those who return the same day, then take the delightful walk along the river bank on the Canada side and view the Falls free of charge.

Thus we have shown that for those who wish and are able to walk, the Falls themselves can be seen with little or no expense. Those coming on the Canadian lines have a free view; those on the American side for 30 cents.

But those who wish to be driven from their station to the Falls must of course pay for the hack. Should they wish to visit the various outlying points of interests in the vicinity, at all of which an admission fee is charged, the bill will necessarily be considerably increased.

TAKE MORE TIME AT NIAGARA

if you would enjoy your visit and save expense. Most people come in on the train and the moment they leave the cars commence rushing from one point of interest to another without any definite idea of where they are going, incur all the expense in a single day that should be distributed over an entire week, and then go home swearing about the "extortions" of Niagara. Niagara Falls and the various places of interest in the vicinity cannot be seen in a few hours. If you would see all, take lodgings at a hotel where the fare is suitable to your means, and then take time for your sight-seeing. If you can afford the luxury of a carriage you can be accommodated at as low a rate as can be obtained at any other place on the continent. If your means will not afford a carriage, there is no reason why you should not adopt the English custom and walk. The distance between the various points of interest is not great, the walks from one place to another are pleasant and safe, and the scenery unsurpassed. [See chapters on Distances and Admission Fees.]

Distances of the Points of Interest from the Falls.

—o—

AMERICAN SIDE.

GOAT Island lies between the Horseshoe and American Falls.

The Three Sister Islands, Luna Island, Bath Island, &c., all belong to the Goat Island group, and are reached only from Goat Island.

Cave of the Winds is behind the Centre Fall and can only be reached from Goat Island.

The Rock of Ages is the huge rock lying in front of the Cave of the Winds.

Prospect Park occupies all the river front between the upper Suspension Bridge and the Falls.

The Shadow of the Rock is behind the sheet of water of the American Fall. It is reached by the Inclined Railway from Prospect Park.

The upper Suspension Bridge is about one-eighth of a mile below the American Fall.

The new Cantilever Bridge is about two miles below the Falls.

The Railway Suspension Bridge is only 380 feet below the Cantilever Bridge, hence two miles below the Falls.

The Whirlpool Rapids is about half a mile below the Railway Suspension Bridge.

The Whirlpool is about one mile below the Railway Suspension Bridge, hence about three miles from the Falls.

The Devil's Hole is about one mile down the river from the Whirlpool, but at this date is not open for visitors.

CANADA SIDE.

The Burning Spring is about one mile above the Falls, at the upper end of Clark Hill Islands.

Clark · Hill Islands are five in number, extending from the Falls about one mile up the river, lying between the main land and Rapids.

Falls View is a point nearly in front of Loretto Convent on the brow of the hill overlooking the Rapids and the Falls, where the Michigan Central trains halt for passengers to view the Falls.

The Museum is only a few rods from the Falls.

Lundy's Lane Battle Ground is about one and one-quarter miles west of the Falls.

New Suspension Bridge about half a mile from the Horseshoe Fall.

The Cantilever Bridge and Railway Suspension Bridge are only 380 feet apart and about two miles from the Falls.

Whirlpool Rapids is only about one-eight of a mile below the Railway Suspension Bridge.

The Whirlpool is about one mile below the Railway Suspension Bridge.

Brock's Monument is at Queenston, about seven miles from the Falls.

DISTANCES OF RAILWAY STATIONS FROM THE FALLS.

Michigan Central, Niagara Falls Station, Canada side, is one-half mile.

Grand Trunk, Niagara Falls Station, Canada side, about two miles.

New York Central, Niagara Falls Station, American side, about one-quarter mile.

Erie, Niagara Falls Station, American side, about three-quarters of a mile.

West Shore, Niagara Falls Station, American side, about three-fourths of a mile.

Lehigh Valley, Niagara Falls Station, American side, about three-fourths of a mile.

Rome, Watertown and Ogdensburg, Niagara Falls Station, American side, about one-quarter of a mile.

THE RAILWAY SYSTEM AT NIAGARA FALLS.

All the lines of railway coming to Niagara Falls centre at the point where the Railway Suspension Bridge and new Cantilever Bridge span the river, about two miles below the Falls, and about one mile above the Whirlpool. Each railway, except the Grand Trunk, has a station nearer the Falls, but they all have one also at this place, in close proximity to each other.

Here there is a town on each side of the river with stores, post office, express and telegraph offices, and with abundant hotel accommodation. The place on the American side is called Suspension Bridge, that on the Canadian side Niagara Falls, (formerly Clifton.)

Visitors should take special notice of this fact, as when at this point, on either side of the river, they are about midway between the different points of interest, the Whirlpool on the one side and the Falls on the other.

Hotel fare here, too, is cheaper than it is nearer the Falls, and the accommodation equally as good.

In the matter of hack hire, carriages can be

obtained at this place as cheaply and as readily as at the stations nearer the Falls.

On the American side a street railway with a five cent fare, runs to the Falls. On the Canada side a charming walk along the river bank is open to those who may not wish a carriage.

Admission Fees and Tolls.

AMERICAN SIDE.

To Goat Island for the day..............$0 50
"   "   " season........... 1 00
" Cave of the Winds, with dress & guide 1 00
" Prospect Park for the day............ 0 25
"   "   "   " season......... 0 75
" Art Gallery, (Prospect Park,)......... 0 25
" Inclined Railway   "   " 0 25
" Shadow of the Rock, with dress & guide 1 00
" Ferry to Canada and Prospect Park.. 0 50
" Electric Light, Prospect Park, extra
    on day or season tickets........... 0 15
" Crossing upper Susp. Bridge, each way 0 25
" Crossing Suspension Bridge, extra for
    one-horse carriage................ 0 35
" Crossing Suspension Bridge, extra for
    two-horse carriage carriage........ 0 50
" Railway Suspension Bridge, over and
    return same day................... 0 25
" Whirlpool Rapids................... 0 50
" Whirlpool........................... 0 50
" Devil's Hole, when open to visitors.... 0 50

CANADA SIDE.

To Burning Springs, including Clark Hill
    Islands.........................$0 50
" Falls,.............................. Free
" Lundy's Lane Battle Gro'd Observatory 0 50
" Museum............................ 0 50
" Crossing upper Susp. Bridge, each way 0 25

"   "   "   "   "   extra for
one horse carriage.................$0 35
" Crossing upper Susp. Bridge, extra for
two horse carriage................ 0 50
" Railway Suspension Bridge, over and
return same day.................. 0 25
" Railway Suspension Bridge, extra for
one horse carriage................ 0 35
" Railway Suspension Bridge, extra for
two horse carriage................ 0 50
" Stone Road toll..................... 0 10
" Whirlpool Rapids................... 0 50
" Whirlpool 0 50
" Brock's Monument.................. 0 25

How to Avoid Being Humbugged

1. Know the name of the station where you will leave the cars.

2. Know how far that station is from the Falls, and what time you have at your disposal for sight-seeing.

3. Decide before arriving at the Falls what places you wish to visit. Ascertain from this Guide how far they are from the Falls, and from each other, and what the admission fee is.

4. Remember no point of interest at Niagara Falls is free, except the Falls themselves on the Canadian side.

5. If you take a carriage, make your bargain with the driver before entering the carriage.

6. If you wish to return, you must make that a part of your contract, otherwise you may be required to pay extra for the return drive. —That is one of the tricks.

7. If you need a hotel, select one where the rates correspond with your means and wants.

Hotels range from one to five do'lars per day.

8. Remember that as the driver is in your service for the time being, he wi'l expect you to pay all fees and tolls unless you specially bargain for him to pay them.

9. If any person should defraud you there is no place on the continent where you can get redress more surely or more readily, if you go direct to the authorities with your grievance. The Ontario Police Force, on the Canada side, and any Justice of the Peace on the American side will afford the stranger who applies to them ample protection.

Rates of Fare Allowed by Law.

FOR THE USE AND HIRE OF CARRIAGES WHERE AN EXPRESS CONTRACT IS NOT MADE THEREFOR:

——— o ———

NIAGARA FALLS, N. Y.

FOR carrying one passenger and ordinary baggage from one place to another in the Village, fifty cents

Each additional passenger and ordinary baggage, twenty-five cents.

For carrying one passenger and ordinary baggage from any point in this Village to any point in the Village of Suspension Bridge, one dollar.

Each additional and ordinary baggage, fifty cents.

Each additional piece of baggage other than ordinary baggage, twelve cents.

Children under three years of age, free.

Over three years and under fourteen years of age, half price.

Ordinary baggage is defined to be one trunk

and one bag, hat or bandbox, or other small parcel.

For carrying one or more passengers, in the same carriage, from any point in this village to any point within five miles of the limits of the village, at the rate of one dollar and fifty cents for each hour occupied, except that in every instance where such carriage shall be drawn by a single horse, the fare therefor shall be at the rate of one dollar for each hour occupied.

TARIFF OF HACKMEN'S CHARGES IN THE TOWN OF NIAGARA FALLS, ONT.

From Railway Suspension Bridge or G T. R. Station to Clifton House, or Falls Ferry, Davis' Museum or Table Rock, or *vice versa* - two horses : one person, $1, and each additioral person, 25 cents; one horse : one person, 75 cents, and each additional person, 25 cents. From Falls Ferry to Davis' Museum, or Table Rock, or *vice versa*, two horses : one person, 50 cents, and each additional person, 25 cents; one horse : one person, 37 cents; each additional person, $12\frac{1}{2}$ cents. From Clifton House to Davis' Museum, Table Rock, Falls Ferry. Niagara Falls C. S. R , or *vice versa*, two horses : one person, 25 cents, and each additional person 25 cents; one horse, same price. From any place in the Town to any other place in the Town excepting as above specified for any distance not exceeding one mile, two horses, one person 25 cents, and each additional person 12 cents; one horse: one person, 20 cents; each additional person, 10 cents ; and exceeding one mile, and not exceeding one and one-half miles, two horses: one person, 37½ cents, two persons 50 cents, and each additional person, 20 cents; one horse: one person, 25 cents, and each additional person, 12½ cents; exceeding one and one half miles, two horses: one person. 50 cents, and each additional person, 25 cents; one horse: one person, 37½ cents, two persons, 50 cents, and each additional person, 20 cents.

TARIFF BY THE HOUR: For two-horse vehicles to be $1.50 an hour; for one-horse vehicles to be $1.00 an hour

TARIFF BY THE DAY: To be $8.00 each day of eight hours, for two horses; and $4.00 per day for one horse.

Optional with passengers to pay the special rates by the hour or by the day.

Any person paying by the hour must pay for one full hour, and after the first hour for no less time than one-quarter of an hour; and any person paying by the day must pay for one full day.

Any person employing a vehicle by the hour and not returning with the vehicle to the place of starting, must allow necessary time for the vehicle to return.

Children between 2 and 10 years of age to pay half fare. Under 2 years of age, free.

Passengers to pay all tolls when hiring any vehicle according to the tariff; but if any driver or owner of any vehicle shall agree to convey any passenger or passengers a certain distance for a certain price at a lesser rate than that allowed by the tarriff, or from one part of the municipality to any other part, at a lesser rate than that allowed by the tariff, and in making such agreement makes no mention of any toll gates on the route, or does not agree that such passenger or passengers shall pay all tolls, then the driver or owner of such vehicle shall himself pay all tolls.

CAUTION.

——o——

SOMETIMES visitors are drawn to a point of interest which they do not care to see and consequently refuse to leave the carriage. Then it frequently occurs that they are told by those in attendance "that it makes no difference whether they get out of the hack or not, they are on private property and will have to pay the fee just the same as though they passed through to the point of interest."

In such cases we would warn you not to be deceived, for there is no law in the land that can make you pay for a point of interest that you do not visit. There is no such private property belonging to any point of interest where this fraud is practiced.

This, however, does not apply to the Burning Spring, as Clark Hill Islands, through which they pass to go to the Spring, belong to the point of interest for which the fee is charged. Parties are therefore subject to the fee when they go on the Islands whether they visit the Spring or not.

——o——

N. B.—There is no person permitted to advertise in this volume for whose reliability we cannot vouch.

www.ingramcontent.com/pod-product-compliance
Lightning Source LLC
Chambersburg PA
CBHW021550270326
41930CB00008B/1447